PSYCHO
PETS

First published in 2006 by

PRION
an imprint of the
Carlton Publishing Group
20 Mortimer Street
London W1T 3JW

2 4 6 8 10 9 7 5 3 1

Design copyright © Carlton
Publishing Group 2006
Text copyright © Trevor Baker 2006

A catalogue record for this book is
available from the British Library

ISBN-13: 978-1-85375-596-5
ISBN-10: 1-85375-596-6

Printed and bound in Singapore

PSYCHO PETS

JUST WHEN YOU THOUGHT
IT WAS SAFE TO GO HOME

PRION

CONTENTS

High

Five!

Have you got the
photo yet, Mr
Attenborough?
My jaw's
starting to ache.

If I was a tortoise shell I'd be invisible right now.

The ghosts
of
budgies past.

Lose the broomstick, old lady.

I only fly business class.

Move it, big guy. You're in front of the telly!

Peek-a-boo!

OK, it's
a deal.
No more
dead mice
in the kitchen
provided you
forget this
vegetarian diet
nonsense.
Let's shake on it.

Look into my eyes, not
around the eyes, and ... you're under!

I killed a whole family
of robins this
morning and still
they call me
'Sylvester the Softie'.

You don't like my singing? Your little Persian didn't seem to mind.

I want to
speak to
my lawyer!

Bunny Boilers

The price of
organic carrots??
Don't get me started!

The lettuce won't be so uppity now.

Disney's first live action picture was going well until the hare ate the rooster.

Listen to 'em down there.
They're at it like rabbits.

DERANGED DOGS

Grandma?
No, I haven't
seen her.

I don't really
have big ears,
do I, Mummy?

Well, it worked for Dumbo!

Nice try but nobody ties this dog up.

Ow! What a place to get a splinter.

No, you put your left leg in, your right leg out ...

After a while 'His Master's Voice' really started to grate.

You've got a grey hair! Keep still, I can get it!

Half-wolf, half-bat, and still
Dracula sold me to the dog track.

All right, darlin'!

Is it
'walkies' already?
What a
terrible bore.

Not many people know this but I was Chewbacca's stunt double.

All right, lads,
last one in the sea is
an ... argggggghhhh!

To begin
with there
were 102
Dalmatians.

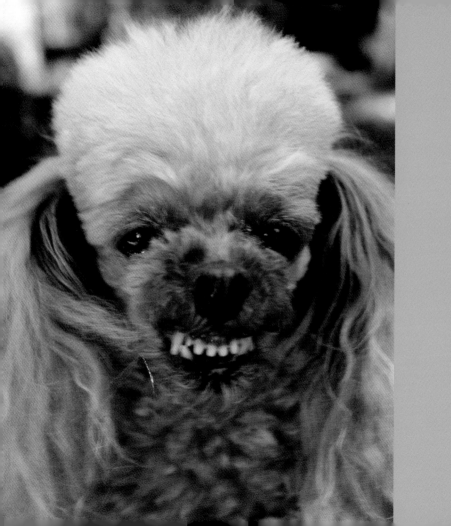

Best in Show
1963

Walkies!

You can put
your little
shovel away.
I'm thinking.

'Just show some fur,' they said. I hope my mum never sees these pictures.

You should see the other guy.

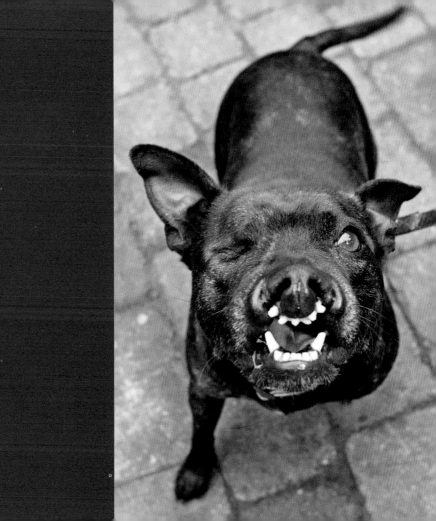

Stand to attention, you 'orrible little shower!

Get orff my land!

'The hills are alive
with the sound of music'

I'm not ugly,
I'm just growing
into my face.

The truth is out there.

'What *is* she wearing, Nicky?'
'Don't be a bitch, Paris.'

We're all dooooomed!

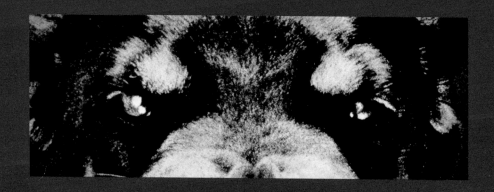

What you lookin' at?

Is that bitch
wearing a waistcoat?
I don't believe it!

Well hello, you're a frisky little thing.

Going somewhere
nice this year, love?

Pardon??

... 98,99,100.

Coming,
ready or not!

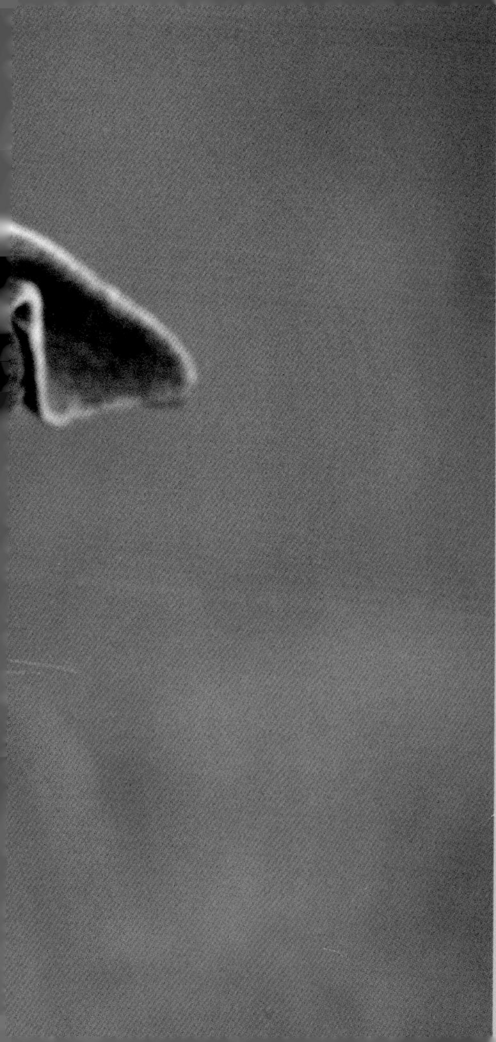

Tell me, Clarice – have the lambs stopped screaming?

CRAZY
HORSES

**Come on,
you know
you want it!**

Red Rum!

Red Rum!

**Heathcliff!
It's me, it's
Cathy, I've
come home!**

**Come back!
You were
going to
tell me
if I've
got halitosis.**

KILLER KITTIES

So I arch my back and suddenly
I'm supposed to be terrifying?

Who spread tuna on the electric cable?

That's not a real mouse but I'm still going to chew its tail off.

Wakey!
Wakey!

I own the sofa now, and the bed, and the carpet, but the litter tray is still yours.

He was trying to
fly even after I
bit his head off!

You ain't seen me, right?

FRIGHTENING FISH

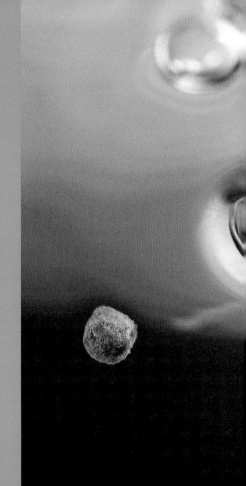

Just When
You Thought
It Was Safe
To Go
Back To
The Fairground

Excuse me, is this the right
way to Weight Watchers?

RABID RODENTS

A nut allergy is a terrible thing

for a rodent to have.

Elevator . . .
Going up!

MAD BIRDs

Achoo!
Achoo!
I'm sure
it's not
bird flu.
I've just
got the
sniffles.

They
put me
in 'ere
'cos I
refused
to sing.

A TETCHY TORTOISE

An hour crawling across the carpet and I'm not even sure this will be worth it.

Picture Credits